MEL C

TUFF ENUFF

Research
Noam Friedlander

Design
JMP Ltd

Photography
The Spice Girls' families
Alex Bailey
Chris Buck
Ray Burmiston
Michael Ginsberg
Adrian Green
Rankin Waddell

Spice Girls Management
Simon Fuller @ 19 Management

Thanks to
Catri Drummond
James Freedman
Sally Hudson
Gerrard Tyrrell

A Zone production

The author and publishers have made every reasonable effort to contact all copyright holders. Any errors that may have occurred are inadvertent and anyone who for any reason has not been contacted is invited to write to the publishers so that a full acknowledgement may be made in subsequent editions of this work.

This book is sold subject to the condition that it shall not by way of trade or otherwise be lent, resold, hired or otherwise circulated without the prior written consent of the Spice Girls in any form other than that which it has been published.

Copyright © Spice Girls Ltd 1997.
All rights reserved.
All photographs reproduced by kind permission of The Spice Girls.

The right of the Spice Girls to be identified as the authors of this book has been asserted by them in accordance with the Copyright, Designs and Patents Act 1988.

Second edition
First published in 1997 by
Zone/Chameleon Books
an imprint of Andre Deutsch Ltd.
a member of the VCI plc Group
106 Great Russell Street
London WCIB 3LJ
in association with19 Management Ltd
Printed in Italy by G. Canale & C. Turin

CIP Data for this title is available from the British Library

ISBN 0223 99324 X

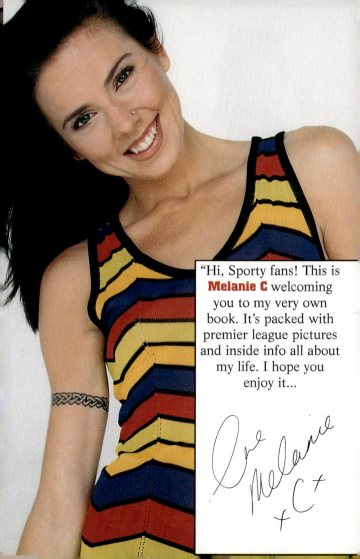

"I'd love to be able to wear skirts like Victoria, but I don't really like my legs."

"I like to exercise, so I go to the gym about five times a week. I run about five miles, do weights and a lot of abdominal work."

"We help each other out to get what we want and we give each other strength."

"I wasn't that interested in education – I just wanted to be a performer. Although I still did quite well – I got four Bs and five Cs in my GCSEs."

"But the one thing I regret is that I didn't do enough revising for my exams. I was really into my dancing and I put all my energy into that, so school work took a back seat."

"I wanted to be a dancer, but I've also always been into football because of where I'm from – everyone from Liverpool loves football. And ballet and football aren't all that different. There's a lot of skill involved in both."

"Where I am now is absolute proof that if you really want something badly enough you can get it."

"When we write a song, we have a huge pad and we just write down ideas – even the most ridiculous silly things. We end up with a big page of phrases and words and put them all together."

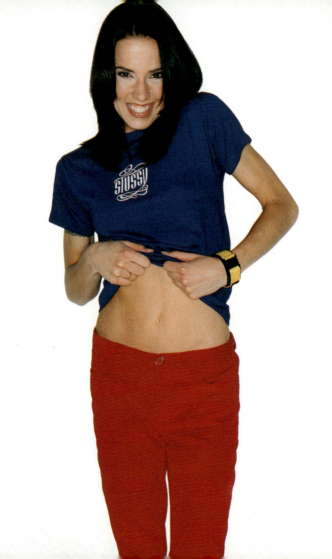

"I'm really shy and quiet, especially if you don't know me, but when it comes to performing, I find it a lot easier."

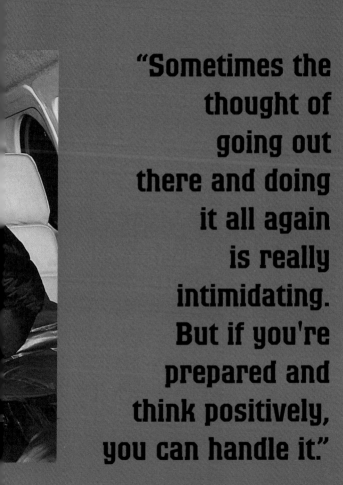

"Sometimes the thought of going out there and doing it all again is really intimidating. But if you're prepared and think positively, you can handle it."

"The fact that I'm in the Spice Girls just proves that if you stick at it and keep working for your dreams and goals, then you achieve them eventually."

"It's good for boys to know about **Girl Power**, too."

"It's getting more and more important to our generation, so why leave the boys out?"

"You have to be cool with yourself. For a long time I, like many other girls, hated the way I looked. You hate your hair and you think you're fat, and you're not happy with this or that and you think all your friends are better than you. That is no way to live."

"It doesn't matter how you get fit, as long as you enjoy it and it's not a chore. At school you've got really good opportunities, 'cos you can be in the football, hockey or netball team, but then when you leave school it gets much more difficult."

"These days I'm eating loads of natural things like pulses and nuts and grains, fruit and vegetables and drinking a lot of water. It's made me feel loads better."

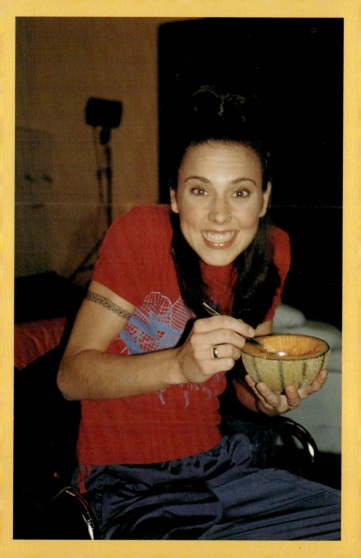

"My make-up bag isn't very good because I'm not really a make-up person."

"I think we're the five luckiest girls on the planet, so that's not too bad, it?"

Mind you, it's really hard work."

"I like being sporty and sometimes I like to be smart, but I always want to feel mobile, like I can do a backflip at any moment."

"I was a bit of a favourite with the music and drama teachers, but there was a maths teacher who didn't like me and kept putting me down into lower and lower sets – I think maths is my worst subject!"

"If you want to feel good, you've got to be good to your body. Just look after yourself."

"I love exercise, and I go to the gym a lot, but I still find that one of the best ways to exercise is to put on my favourite tunes and jump around like a nutter."

"When I was spring cleaning my flat before we went to America, I put all my track suits together. It's really scary opening up the wardrobe now, because there's nothing but track suits in there – every different colour of track suit you can get!"

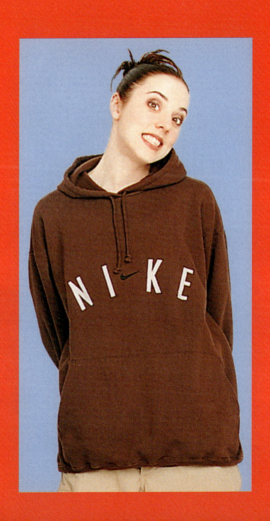

"Sometimes I wear smart hipster trousers and little tank tops so you can see my tattoos. I may wear high heels for special occasions, but I'm usually in trainers."

"I'm rubbish at putting make-up on, but I look dog rough without it. I don't mind that normally, but now I'm having my picture taken all the time, I have to worry more about my appearance."

"The best thing about being a girl nowadays is that you can do lads' stuff too and that's cool."

"No matter how tired I feel, I know I'll never stop performing."

"I'm very shy when I meet people."

"Eyes are the windows of the soul. I think you can show whatever you're feeling through your eyes."

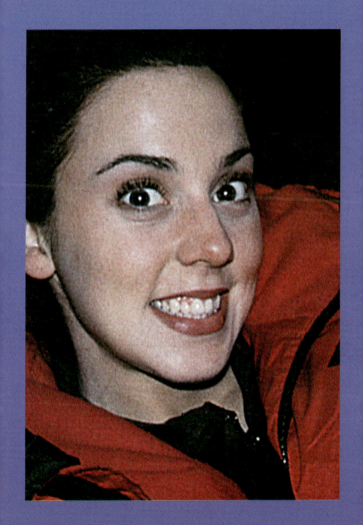

"I never have any expectations and just take it all as it comes. Every thing we do just seems to get

bigger and bigger, but all I can think is that we're five dead normal girls just writing a few tunes."

"We've all got to look after ourselves when we're about to sing live. We can't go partying too much, because everything affects your vocal chords. So we have to get plenty of rest and take it easy."

"Ever since I was a kid I said, I wannabe a pop star, but people never took me seriously."

Thanks for reading my book!

Love Melanie C ✕

GET THE SET! FOUR MORE **OFFICIAL** MINIBOOKS TO COLLECT

SPICE GIRLS OFFICIAL PUBLICATIONS